Little "g" God Grows Tired of Me

Aby Kaupang

Little "g" God Grows Tired of Me

Published by SpringGun Press
Denver, CO
www.springgunpress.com

Little "g" God Grows Tired of Me
©2013 by Aby Kaupang
All rights reserved

Printed in the United States of America
Second Printing

ISBN 978-0-9832218-6-9

Cover art by Nora Sturges
Design by Erin Costello

Distributed to the trade by Small Press Distribution *(spdbooks.org)*

Grateful acknowledgment is made to the editors and staff of the following presses who generously published many of these poems: *Best New Poets, Caketrain, Dusie, Fourteen Hills, Interim, Lamination Colony, Laurel Review, Matter, Parthenon West, Ruminate, Scantily Clad Press, Tebot Bach,* and *Verse.*

Thank you to my friends for their vision and pens: Dan Beachy-Quick, Logan Burns, Micah Cavaleri, Gordon Hadfield, Chloe Leisure, Marty Moran, Sasha Steensen, and Kevin Ward.

Thank you to the editors at SpringGun Press for their keenest eyes, measures of humor, enduring patience and most of all their faith in the work: Erin Costello, Derrick Mund and Mark Rockswold.

for Matthew, Elias and Maya

Contents

1 Reliquary

12 The Massacre Room

27 Scenic Fences

50 Cupboard of Silk and Sackcloth

67 Innumerable Houses

77 Egress

Reliquary

Tender such reliquary

Threat is a vacant place. A cove to sleep in. A solidarity of no-motion. I want to sleep

there. All my mighty babies are sleeping. Here. Heavy. Violence is always on the shore and away. There is a deep mean dam away.

In the float of partials, rivers feed in retro. Bodies float within themselves. A fly rod hooks a fissure. Your body's best this way and thick—treading densities, we best maneuver when unzipped.

Tender

come   plumb's what
I want
    you

in tension
    tents circle   wretch
in a ditch
    I crouch

ships glide over
bruised curtains

      wreck to them
I will
    come

Tender the definition

young and vulnerable of tender age

        youngwife
        could not take her actions valuably

so is an offer of monies
of service an obligation or a bid

easily crushed and bruised

        {could and should have noted}
        it did help the rest   the temper
        to eat the buffalo   to grateful

the frost too seemed colder   more "complicated"

        September's echeveria not yet mulberry tipped
        and gloved up   her wrists   nerves
        unnerved   prep for November

natatorium: the pool   nautical: the ship

    who hearts sad songs
    this is not a sad song

considerate and protective

    a solicitous mother
    was tender {is the night}
    is the night   rest
    unto her children

who are likely to heel easily
    a: the crank
    a {extensible} : under sail

In our unbuilt bodies beyond de Kooning's river door

I am a room rising—a rising that will not be a room.

I am being visited for aways and nears and in unbuilt chambers we appear. Here in the slightly scene vanish is not spill is not built is forever still on the sill of the banks. Here we emerge and disappear.

"Flocks of amber geese nest in warm tombs of your side." You've mouthed what you won't rumor even. So we tuck our sublimations inside envelopes.

This is a found chamber of skin—I stay here. You pace holloways of its bones. You hide all your fine creations forged tight as screws in cartilage boxes sunk in grooves. Here no sofa no lamp no tin by a no stove. Only reeds and blue and sometimes scrape.

Do you know what the geese are plotting inside me? All the birds have holloways beyond where we have ever peered and little fingers turning knobs on roofs to exiting streams. You are telling me of cant-ing: we are strumming all our plumes.

I am weaving in the dimness by the banks.

This is the tunnel and this is the runner and this is the roller steel and rusting as dense as a limb. Here we're ambushed in the thistles. You weave a willow with a willow and wind them 'til I'm gone.

There are windows in the breezeways of our ribcage. There are shutters bombing open. There are envelopes in tiny palms in beaks of amber spilling. There are geese shaking skywings. They are flying in and back and they are pulsing for our babies curved here in my marrow.

Strom hopes {he's a feathery thing}

Strom needs everyday
everyday in _____ to be a good day

for a deal. Ours:
the stray and the struth and the slight.

                           A new deal.

He who buys into segregation buys
Modernity:
                 the front porch taser
                 the forehead tent
                 the nano comfort

Nobody knows it but Thurman's so sad.

The beginning of love, he mused,
is a feeding tube on the sly.

He fingers a name in the soot.

emergency is slow seep. not splay. the body on the sofa. {splay spread}. the body on the sofa. {interior seeping}. two drove. on the sofa. to Chiron. overnight.

Infant fissure:

        still
        in the cave—give her
        dimness   scarlet   saltspray prayers
                                        and push

        the heavenly
        caravans

        into a sea

        brine-heart
        you know distant
        gulls pile masts   wrecked
        seaships and blue and where

        astral wheels
                        aren't monuments of wrath

        writhe then
        the sea is full

        it lures my betters to dim and splay

                what pearl
                   what pearl—

Sundays are inconvenient   god

as value absolutes away   the dailies
who deliver the enterprise

call: when does a product available

                              in the night
seen and not
touched   mannequins respond

showcase in showcase beyond
pane and glass
praise for a station so apt

restaurateurs sidewalk into morning

much of advertisement wins me
the vendor's package angers the vendor
who is angry often

response: when a catalogue touches back
gets tattoos   makes Kodak the daddies

who borrow their inheritance
on the weekend

            I hang   and I am   a part

It takes a pillage to sing a Strom song

A village to make a nation
gross. The National Product is gross.

Strom looks at it
from both sides—two sides—now
from X's and O's and still
somehow it's personal
illusions Strom recalls.

Style? Still Strom. Mael____.
Whoa. Down now boy.

There's a pony in Strom,
a stallion among us.

The Massacre Room

***

This is the way you changed the river: you put your body in it. This is the way I learn to drown: I weave my body out.

Trout in the deep can grow quite heavy and pressure often spoons the concrete sill. Somewhere on between I slip. {Such reliquary of foreheads}. Sand on my towel, trowel where it should be. It's why the trout are in the trees. Why the river weans itself.

This is what I do in nothing: I stare at the mica that watch at you. By the splay of flint on the bed, you don't even sense it.

So autumn. Not always an action. I am humming your desire to autumn. In the building of a fire you mouth *rest*. I am never very hungry anymore.

Massacre

curves—
leans low
a portal house

early mage
terminals spill so tidally slow

Something pale unearths shovels of light

something's straining candles in this field

the father and I   we renew silence
but are late with it

Pity's bound in twine   gathered now
I'm starring   starring at a made-body of a once-him

why do I want at anyone here
his rib in my palm

I can't pry it out

when the plows pull   grip by
tendrils of rain   mud cocoon
across my arms

the ground wells purple

perhaps it is that blackness flows through soil
or I am reckoning panes of un-sight
or cross-hatched light combusts when branches merge

something's heaving beneath this carpet of plains

something's flying after darkness
darkness hang me in your shed

Alone amid the fires

                                        smoke and mirrors/
                                        mirrors and smoke

and the camp songs and the ponderosas

                                            my love's rosy lips
                                            afloat in the brine

thin Strom wonders at Libra imbalanced in the skies

A loner refurbishes some tangle in the loveseat

How tonight is language anything but tincture. Punctured. Lovely too—the loner refurbishes some tangle in a loveseat. A river forced under returns. It wants to undrown. To introduce its milkteeth. So invisible,
the clay hours groan.

When stillness slips to gift's visage, a crash slithers, an estimated reach exhales.

>	tounges and fiddleheads
>	curling find
>	fiddleheads tongues
>	unfurling come

The loner is an awful salesman. Actually, the condition of water pre-diluvian. Its heaving, drawn up. Leafing.

Lonely waters.

Suddenly flowing and wronged. Lovely, the respondent, you, are the vowel spilling out—

He who believes in you futures

I get up   my friend is Brazilian   I admire her
we are not friends   actually
her strategy in dailies is remarkable
the husband says it then scribes it in absence

many important objects are hazardous
inconvenient   actually   my other friend
in this world joins
the army   has never seen
Central Park   I can imagine going

nowhere together   weightless
and many are the pennies in grocery bags
maybe we are all important
left
       I bought my ideas
elsewhere   the husband does not
budget anxiety   he will go
to New York   and again
the Army   will not   see it

who will slow   every hour
                        a war poem

My son is born of me. Women give births {take away   take out   our sons}. Who is full of misery? When they're up they're up and when they're down they're down. Hi ho the flower. This world is not our home.

Weary in spring at the heater

perhaps to fast the body is to move
the furniture before the body
collapses   beamless
bone on itself

every May the want
seed   every year the rental
frosts to wither a start-ling

these skins are irrelevant   I want
to not touch but to fence a touching

to unpause the skirmishlessness
the union itself never presenting

      do you have any
idea what the day is about

the dying trapped in the idea of their death not the loss itself
this the loss
        I am pregnant

with Nameless to Nameless forgiving

I rent   reside
in the contract of un-ness often

yet there is still a desiring to walk ridges for the inbetweens dawns dusking
long lines unhindered in towns in gardens on hillsides I love them I must them

Nameless I am sorry I
don't know own

can I say I need *catholic*
with connotations stretched and deferring

I am poisoned from August
and leases   my mind
records in charcoal and charts and I
think today is vaster

than the rental
the chipping of floors   the wretch of the basemented neighbor
who blasphemes through heating vents open   whoring

have I gobbled
too fully Nameless
the idea of me—I
don't taste me ever

how do I plead
something   someone
generous   un-reciprocitious
in this rental this vent

to grow is to nourish is to submit to element
to un-claim

the skin is to starve and not take
not lease not pay not debt the pores out

space always the need of rafters and walls

Strom days are roses

       We are bury Strom.

It's a way of keeping the flesh
at bay.
       Stromland security.

A baby cries herself out.
We acquire a bridge. Singe
a bridge. We are older.
No rest no peas in the queue.

       Listen to the Thurman on the mount.

He says to her back *should we
get tattoos you and* to the door
I together?

       Stromming my heart with her fingers.

She would throw rugs.

       Strom diddy Strom
       diddy Strom {3x}

Another round of goat songs.

Nothing splashes in

natural boundaries seize
cease from doing so—"no"

        no blood
        vessel splay
        no play
        no river
        no river veers course

curse   then   the   world   is   slow

slow: lets us {rivers vessels chambers} leak

August is so subsumable

a result of interpolations   the edge
of yucca razing   queued

behind initiative   endings   and all
all around   god
replays initiatives

blessed be the juncture

introductions hoop   crew as
seedpod   quiescence

        such history
         avant-garde

before the hogback
then before seep   then   *grant it*
before generosity
the corporeal   fraying

into one measure of trailer
demarcated   by ditches   drytops

        selah

the bone where bloom
posts for locative confidence

        selah

One birdhouse per truncation
groves the lawn and alpenglow.
A soldier vanises. The aviary—
what a beautiful bird-circus
the family encrusts on marble.

Polyphony from the husband

Wife you are courting a requiem

and seems you have
bought   seems all already
but what
            bought is all directorially
thrown

Wife   seems best
                        to eternal the interior
to reach the watching
jades   they've toppled their pots
again   make them
            sign something   *laughwife*

greener   duller   their spill
than your purchase extensibled

de-thaw the lamb
holy   holy   holy Wife

Scenic Fences

a room evacuated

kept   unfilled has room for seven times the demons   seven times the stilled the selved   the leaving fences

in the air   white fledglings   ladders unfurl domes contract   and here   scenic in the field   wave demarcations at the missing when the runaway can't scale the mind   when the fence is scenic when a blue kettle screeching is the last soldier in the house is me hummingbird scratching   when sidewalks refract dawn's fight-driven dreams to meridians to tombs to fingers to juleps bracelets cast ghostlights in the kitchen in slant in late in I am turning alright now becoming a room for books and hued tables in a woven night a pilled waking and visionful night

the body   {that other body you
respond to—the one you reap}

                              refuses to wake
                              writes *grieve*

in the rainbed   the basalt   the mobile
choking over the baby's crib

field called open house   all the banners unraveling
all pointing a way

recall the viewers
the linen lined egalitarians white waiverers pinned to—

        wait

not enough delineation: I

don't see

don't plough
don't furrow
don't lamb
my rivers each spring a finale   requiemed

two *hail our fathers*
one *te adoro*

birthright   lambing eye   my portable
infirmity   you pin assumptions to ingredients
summon all your rakes for usurpation   you who
make a father remake your son   you're a self   so
take take take   the whole poured family shopping
Sunday   bathe them in the hot springs   rend
something

a century of employments rolling over have
left the viewers watching the witness

—pinned to what their wire is   where it
fixates in whose womb   mean and wild the
belly cords each singularity to the notion that
one could be generous   one could   look
closely in your pantry

return the body {the one you
resound to} lose it once

and leave

be sad at the demolition of *house*

sweep   then sweep
and let—
            if the underbelly shows
echoes at empathy—
                        let let let
any worth resist markets

I will give you a new name and the name in truths is *Perfect* to do other things:

build a hummingbird dome   wear a mean hat
erase the harbourers and kepts   dictate traffic
in the garden land   loose clod

let let let   {white triangles slapping a
window}

squirrels and sweet peas climb into your
dovecote

surrender then is   egalitarian
prolific
expansively exhumable

tubas in a funereal parade

blessed are the   multitudinous
for my flesh   on this morning
confetties the temple

                                                    {him}

three addresses for the outcome:

if I lose them all   me
~~if I am unclear or echoes are loudest~~   addendum:
                                                         impossible
if proudly cohesive

here the troops never gave birth against the enemy

ménage-a-toi

the bodies beside
the body   {you
sometimes}   and lying
there and trying
accidentally appear too

misaddress invitations for
other men's pockets

the missings slipped through
the fence was illusory
the ladder unparsed

how fall of me to eclipse the viewers

rent
rent
rent

if there is no one beyond the veil

the cast is not the monstrous

shadow

belly button in the bell jar
sunlight on the mourning sill
something

squirms through

sweep   then   sweep   if we
don't leave tonight   please {we
are still   here} or if
we do {we are here
still}
        leave   leave the door
unlatched

when the mug is bottomless   when I   leave
the table through it   when I pass people
coming in   when I find them in my mouth
when they hammock in my incisors   won't
change the bathwater   when they do and
when they heave it down my neck and
raccoons lap me up   I turn   wreck into
dim shadows   whom I've kept   whom I
covet   whom I cannot speak

and when they would wander I've caged them

so many kingdoms come without joy
leaving impossibles the motion

nesting beyond here   goodbye and goodbye
and day don't come back or day I give and
cant and give

count my unlessings
while casing is wanting
is swept

let out the simpers   let the invites   unfolding
appear

Cupboard of Silk and Sackcloth

***

I float your baby inside me.

For winters, it never comes out. So much pushing at the river, every cast a nearly tight wire into several nearly selves. I can nearly swim here. I know nearly nothing.

Some six-foot fish suspends it in the elms and we are breathing so breathingly.

We slither. The trout too slither. They are slapping down from leaves. They are slipping through the gunk.

Congealing low the banks are fumed. Currents thick today. My little baby's bigger—than me—snake's bigger belly than me. Zippers are jammed with gunk and the when-ness of rapid solemnity.

This is the way you changed the river: I cast my body in it.
This is the way I stay the shore: you proffer it to loaners.

I brought little into this house and it is certain
I can carry nothing out. I gave and took
{Goodwill® to all}; blessed be my new name.

Apologia

1. deliquesce

   a standard passively deliquesces

               like femininity
                   {a region I care for}

is intimate then
like exclusion   like water   like thighs   sliding beyond
reservoirs   and rest   like

                         2. sufferage

                     the extent of displacement prolonged

                         {alt., endure}
                             {non alt., opt}

                                 a rule is
               radiance   like moxie and disclosure

             {these are words   we have
             said   the laying across I do}

             blame-worthiness is restrained
                                reticent

             possibly {and possibly}
                     it is useless
                     as I am useless

3. at the cart

    I work in the mall   I vend silvery chains from Chihuahua
    my boss is very {alt., *very very*—} suave

    he's a real boss and named Carlos

    he is like jewelry

        how good to have a name
        a name means nothing
        but punctuality and armlessness

                              Carlos is an aesthete   I am

                                                    useless
                                           useless as words
                                                are useful
                                                    mostly

                            in fusions and communal deliquescence

4. thighs

    cry *thighs*
            —it's not thigh bodies
  {alt., dissociates} that fumble me

but their occlusion and region   their visions further-past visions

5. away

    at the reservoir
    discretions

  don't concern me

      {think pace and pause

      and majesty} like mountains

reflecting a water or the act   {alt., communion}   between
mountain and mountain reflected

   is mighty

not the mountain nor the reflection but the two together at last:

      a writer
      and the jewels of Chihuahua

        peddled in the low slung ceilings of commerce   illuminated
                                  for holy days for holiday for

                  {silent night}

          this air deliquesces in translation

6. the arbors

    are suffocating in the storefront   they are absent
    in the storefront   they are on a T-shirt

            like bravado   lacked   a mirror more
            memorable than the touching of myself
            most women do   exhaust me {alt., femininity}

            this is moxie

7. spectrum

    is pseudonym for region
    this is   mimesis | meioses | bad breath

    is a function   clearly
    of waking up
    with anyone

    a mimosa forest   a specified forest
    is real wilting
            with a face to the water
            with a face the wilted forest

    and a face watching into the face in the forest

            and water resplendent

            {obv., it doesn't
            matter now

8. if I write}

    arbor or *mountain* or *mall cart* or *very*

    mimesis has succeeded
       in bowing a trinity
                         radiance

    pings from boundaries impinged

9. I is useless in the dung
   of words that name

         my name
      is brachial   stretchingly itinerant

                      confession {I am intimate}:

                          I do care highly
              for the naming of ranges {singular}
                  the centrifuge I cast home

                          I the demarcator
                      the vendor merciful
    the one-eyed migrant moxied in your treethrone

                        I never went back
              to collision or the waters
      or pardons over concrete stairs of men

                          this is a burial

10. *apologia*

word on top
of the word

I'm sorry then
I said it

Love: I do not love poems

how many love poems   Love
can be written to love   myriads
of women   places
before they are   not
love poems   Love
but proofs you
         hold

        easily
slipping
definitions of love—

               O sad one

O tree tree foreign place
material {*clay or iron or tongue*}
and dance   limbs

a tired tread of their walk to the door

                         {surprised you?

a man walks out   did he
ever walk in   I mean   deeply in}

of their heals on the plank while the tragic
pirate pokes and pities {the self pirate} and
fills his pirate dance card and slides his sad eye easy
lovin' pirate peg up a skirt—
                          O clay O city O beach
O herb O sweat O sound

heart whore

                                      {but what more is
                                                a life
                                               a love
                                                poem
                                               Wife?

O pet name
O novel O tree O limb
Oh Ohh Ohhhhhh O

If grace, then—

most sins can be traced
most track-able
to social elements, say   domination

but love in the shadow forces a total stripping

decreate is to unmake   to generous
a body   a back   to Nameless

the name retracted
comes in suffering

young girl balances   counterweights
the whole universe   weighing
the tender of past and future tenders
a lure for
        {quick someone
        call a
        Euphoria}

and in the bare instant of renunciation
hook line and

salvation
        plums at the peak
too brief in the limb to base
at the trunk

of these no human should be
deprived

when the worker doesn't lie
she touches heaven

       that relative
and mixed good thing

Heavier light leaves

in enormous all wings
greatly flows off somewhere

I knew good back then
the man praised

flows late   is grievy
               saint fall
Fall rouse us

my made   it's made well
unlike us
ground between things
soulsky resembles seascold

my Heavy—

Still: thwife'n it

Rituals: are what we're all inside of, prayer flag canaries, familial masks, anniversary sheers, "women—they're always writing about birds"

Bibere: ristretto, the whites {grapefruit or butterscotch notes}, dark and malty/malty and drinky, Emergen-C, little mouth, dos dead guys, aged sumatra, abstinence

Magazines: *Craft, Gastronimica, NewYorker, 1913, Newsweek, Vogue, Highlights, Hotel I5*

redux reduxed: _____ = thief twice
_____ = thusband
_____ = I will not dye hair

{a. thwife   b. thousands of husband   c. thouse}

Alterity upon alterity: {we are more or less the simian} thusband's hair and baby's nerves grow thin, minutia, winter sprouting, see SPD

see jane: see desire, see jack, see the landfill fill, see what peaches w/he dare to eat, see-saw and screw

desire: to snip the mobius, jellyfish grace, to 6 o'clock dine, to otter-it-up, to 6 a week workdays, ascension{s various}

Exfoliate: lavender oil + sugar or cocoa + sugar + unscented oil, "marriage and vine plants—approach with merciless pruning shears"

Hack-a-hack-a-hacka-a
yuk yuk yuk

our obvious poems in big "G" god's ear

God's eye: a long canopic drive south, Humboldt, can't see the forest for the lo{n}gging, a redwood deck, my redneck roots,

ancient darlingtonia   I love you

say serious. "series"

mouth mouth mouth mouth. you know.   :mouth
                                    what comes next

Innumerable Houses

I inhabit innumerable houses

remembering I am changed

observation
does this
        I am the *others* house
stop at the *others* house fill your mug and head
with straw
        leave {alt., lease}

the marginalia of absence eternally returns

commodification is here to replicate
I am always already incriminated
uniquely   this is purchase / I am type

see shopgirl, see domestic, see anyone *blurry* {?}

I consider *others* at museums and in storefronts when I am long in the city. In an ocular, two principals collide: recognition {leads to grace} and observation {leads to alteration} and a third hallway I am sure of: infinite uncertainty {which *is* sadness}.

the mirror made of flesh

the manna and the fish

{retraction}

repeat bouts and grief
sometimes {alt., later} a diagnosis
claims   flowcharts   a future probabled

I recognize a face today

is an urn's opening
a fairly stable portico
janus of nourish and dye

"g" is a master amputator

{faking it, pleasured}   her X
like my X   {faking it, pleasured}

in remembrance
the skin   / is
an urn   /   of finite modality

in resemblance
of me   / grieve

in exchange
I inhabit innumerable houses

your "body
            in jeopardy"

is {alt., leads to}

obligation

I am the city considering others the museum and storefronts. Two principals enter an ocular bar, one is named Grace and the other Grief. I hire them both to pace the holloway. Grace is insistent uncertainty and sadness. Grief, her mi{ni}ster.

commodification is there to replicate and I do
it uniquely for such a hype girl for such a type
girl I'm always emaciated

                                      this is my cred
                                      to recognize a face
                                      is a urinal opening a fair port
                                      all fake and pleasury

I love to hum *fake and pleasury*
                fake and pleasury

Egress

**

Is there any tender here?

We are all desirous. We swim away.
We carry a canyon in us.

Elms drown. We drowned. Such bondage in a fissure.

Below the silt the water's zipper bars back a—
braces all my—

If River runs
its river fingers
cross fontanels and fissures

then what I want is sleep—

Tender submariner:

latched   drenched in flames
my maple tree in a seaship

                                    some breaths
in deep trenches
                        brim over
shatter
            plunge my sirens low

A man will murder a man and he will

call it fashion. The industrial park—it has nothing to do with you. Brethren do you sleep with doors, do you sleep with ennui about you?

Who were we and when
did we say
the light is softer in here?

There's a girl in a lavender headband. She's waiting and Brethren she's waiting. Is there something unrare to assume? Some name to guide her languor? Rarely anyone's sure of first fire.

This lamp is a nasty-ish hue.

So pillage.

It takes a pillage—
and no man
is lesser no Sir
not your equal unequal.

        This lamp is a brethren of Eve.

1. The failures of Thwife being multitudinous

        lending often the gully
        a flight   a lacked coin   a falcate scar
        the cliff rings in familiar lines

        she's productive Anger
        conflating and makes
        Thusband a pretty
        pain of knit and old

        the lyric of presents' tragedy

2. Ways that I hurt and all of the ways to

                                      Henry,

                                      the day's so gold and I'm
                                      just unfit for doing the thing.

                                      Thusband is not how this went.

                                                      2/18/xx

3. 21st c. mondegreens

                 Thwife: thief twice
                 Thusband: thousands of husband

                 Thouse: I will not die hair

4. You might like gypsy

        some women heart houses
        and they are all going out

        of business   she hearts mirage
        so hostile now   the camel

        on the drive making happy
        buying from above

        and north that river those elms
        th' always never
        a sign her head's got nothin'

        she hearts what she
        chose him   she
        wants to be his house

Within the slaughtering shed

Now unpurposed, lofty, dim and elm, it's pocked by decades of December's hail. Fever pigeons blush beneath its crumpled hour. Enough or all their coo cannot submerge the splintering rafters' dusty places, reliquary traces forming spaces. I can't exact a suitable payment from my palm.

I'd anticipated winter here but winter here recalled itself and longed for five long years. To advance then now from loss and quiet and reverence of cost? I do not wonder at the elegance of lack. There is no expenditure of anger, the motion of ferocity and fear, when it is free in the slaughter shed. When it is shredded in the beaming where the cooing wings nest.

Notes of dusted light make pilgrimages from choired rafters through the dimness, the ploughing shears, the cardboard barrels of feed and mice that are and are not inside themselves. And I am knotted in the beams and a bloom is on the floor. Christliness

perpetual empties to the earthy floor—not formed of dirt or clay or hardened irrigants of ditch and field but something finer, deep and silky—perpetual. Light hazes pallid on errancy, descends beneath the swaying creak of wrought pulleys, wheelbarrows, rat burrows. And light

cracks in from where branches slog in March, where winter melts to gift in slanted afternoon, to here where air is choir and choirs disparate—a dirge, a hymn, a requiem, natival, *excommunicatio*—pigeons knotted in the blush.

Little "g" god grows tired of me

this my drowning day

they say I seem wrung
what a drench
of tongue I am

me a tender haunting in the glass beneath the waves
me a blessed peacemaker
me tonguing Chiron for his skiff
me my own My Heavy—

                Tentacle on lip

Après toi, le Deluge Cochineal

crimson around things
delicious   luscious

wheel barrow to calla lip

it seemed a fine coffer
carnine in winter snow   we were curious
how we hadn't known   retrospected
we'd been left in it   fainting there while the skilled moons
circled by lilies   ice crowns   pine bough
pressed stiffly into our grave

russian doll red wall
the way we start a fire

in the year of solutions
we painted it red

we bought it red
our friends and we   spoke red

we couldn't stop the ferrous wake

drifts slight enough for hibernation
wide enough to conceal the slope

slept heavily

asphyxiated the chirring roots

the intermezzo of two lives *près* and *après* of both

arise

red mouthed
cherried

About the Author

Aby Kaupang, author of *Little "g" God Grows Tired of Me* (SpringGun Press, 2013), *Absence is Such a Transparent House* (Tebot Bach, 2011) and *Scenic Fences | Houses Innumerable* (Scantily Clad Press, 2008), has had poems appear in *FENCE, La Petite Zine, Dusie, Verse, Denver Quarterly, The Laurel Review, Parthenon West, PANK, Aufgabe, Fourteen Hills, Interim, Caketrain,* and others. She holds both a Master's of Fine Arts in Creative Writing and a Master's of Occupational Therapy from Colorado State University. She lives in Fort Collins with the poet, Matthew Cooperman and their two children. More information can be found at http://www.abykaupang.com.